SPECTACULAR
SYDNEY

Published by
Woollahra Sales and Imports
Unit 6, 32–60 Alice Street, Newtown, New South Wales, Australia, 2042
Phone: (02) 9557 8299 Facsimile: (02) 9557 8202

Produced by
Murray David Publishing
Publishing Director: Murray Child
Marketing Director: David Jenkins
35 Borgnis Street, Davidson, New South Wales, Australia, 2085
Photographs © Geoff Higgins, 2004
Text: © Murray David Publishing, 2004
Published edition © Murray David Publishing, 2004
Text by Dalys Newman
Printed in Indonesia

ISBN 1 876553 31 6

SPECTACULAR
SYDNEY

PHOTOGRAPHS BY GEOFF HIGGINS
TEXT BY DALYS NEWMAN

WOOLLAHRA

INTRODUCTION

Sophisticated, colourful and energetic, Sydney is Australia's largest city and one of the most beautiful cities in the world. From its humble beginnings as a convict settlement studded with tents and crossed by bullock tracks, it has grown into a dynamic, vibrant and modern metropolis. It is the largest manufacturing centre in Australia, the capital city of New South Wales, focal point of the State's road, rail and air services, the leading commercial and banking centre and home to almost a quarter of the national population.

Covering an area of 12 407 square kilometres, it is a city of great diversity. Long stretches of golden sand and rolling surf, and immense expanses of unspoilt bushland border intensive high-rise precincts and sprawling suburbia. Three rivers meander through the metropolitan area, making Sydney truly a city centred around aquatic activities. To the west are the majestic Blue Mountains, to the south the glorious landscapes of the Southern Highlands and to the north the holiday mecca of the Central Coast.

The brightest star in the city's firmament is, of course, its harbour. Covering an area of 55 square kilometres, this most magnificent body of sparkling water is always alive with pleasure craft, ferries and commercial shipping. The soaring sails of the Opera House and the imposing arch of the Harbour Bridge are the jewels in the harbour's crown.

Much of the city's heritage has been preserved. The Rocks area contains many reminders of Sydney's convict past and the Central Business District is dotted with beautiful nineteenth-century buildings, mingling with modern glass and concrete structures to give the city its unique character. Despite vibrant growth, Sydney has kept a proud eye on its heritage as the site of first European settlement in Australia.

Stunning natural features and the sunny climate, combined with the city's pioneer past and today's bustling, cosmopolitan atmosphere make Sydney a place of zest, vitality and great beauty.

Overleaf: Sydney's icons — the soaring sails of the Opera House and the arching Harbour Bridge. **Title page:** Sydney's old town, the Rocks area, is dwarfed by the looming high-rise buildings. Narrow terraces line many of the twisting streets and tiny cobbled laneways crisscross the area. **Above:** Pleasure craft crowd the sheltered marinas and moorings at Rose Bay, one of the city's exclusive eastern harbour-front suburbs. **Opposite:** The mighty El Alamein Fountain in Kings Cross was built in 1961 to commemorate the part played by Australian forces in the siege of Tobruk and the battle of El Alamein.

Opposite: A triumph of modern architecture, the Sydney Opera House was designed by Danish architect Joern Utzon and completed in 1973 at a cost of over $100 million. It was voted first among the seven wonders of the twentieth century by readers of *The Times* in 1991.

Right: The clean lines of the Opera House incorporate a complex of more than 900 rooms including the 2700-seat Concert Hall, Opera Theatre, Playhouse, Drama Theatre and Cinema as well as restaurants and recording and exhibition halls. It is covered by more than a million tiles that catch the sun's rays, shimmering with the changing play of light across their surface.

Below: Sydney at night — city tower blocks stack up behind a brooding Opera House. Although called an opera house, the building fulfils a multifunctional role, being used for symphony concerts, variety shows, opera, ballet, drama, movies, chamber music and conventions.

Above: Crowds gather to watch outdoor performances on the steps of the Sydney Opera House. The hub of the city's cultural life, all manner of activities are offered at this stunning venue.

Opposite: More than a thousand people of about forty nationalities, all resident in Sydney, perform at the spectacular Folkloric Festival held annually at the Opera House.

Opposite: Opalescent evening light silhouettes one of the massive granite pylons of the Harbour Bridge. Forty thousand pieces of granite went into making these pylons which are purely decorative, only their lower halves supporting the 30 000 tonnes of steel which provide the bridge's structural support. The pylon closest to the Opera House contains a lookout and museum.

Left: The Harbour Bridge, with a total length of 1149 metres, was for many years the longest suspension bridge in the world. It crosses azure waters to connect the City of Sydney to the high density, high-rise satellite city of North Sydney and the sprawling northern suburbs.

Below: Opened in 1932, at a total cost of $19 million, the Harbour Bridge is held together by around six million rivets. The arch span reaches 503 metres, deck height above the water is 59 metres and the crown of the arch towers 134 metres above sea level.

Previous pages: Affectionately known as 'the coathanger', the Harbour Bridge at night is a magically lit landmark.

Opposite: In front of the Australian Maritime Museum floats the unmanned lightship Carpentaria, built in 1917. These ships were once moored above submerged shoals and shifting sand-banks to warn ships of the navigational hazard.

Right: Pavilions of the Harbourside Festival Market-place at Darling Harbour house over two hundred specialty shops, restaurants, cafes and food outlets.

Below: The Novotel Hotel dominates the skyline at the Darling Harbour Complex surrounding Cockle Bay on the western edge of the city. Initiated as part of the 1988 Bicentennial programme, the complex cost in excess of $1800 million.

Above: A trip down memory lane — paddlewheelers, once the backbone of commerce in Australia, last plied the waters in the 1880s. A cruise on MV *Showboat*, a modern paddlewheeler carrying 300 passengers, is one of the many ways to enjoy Sydney Harbour.

Opposite: The Rocks — birthplace of a nation. Despite a backdrop of towering highrises and the bustling harbour transportation, the Rocks area remains the focal point of old Sydney. Today the area has a very relaxed atmosphere with plenty of cafes and busker entertainment. In this picture the replica of HMS *Bounty* is moored.

Opposite: Work and play — view to the Central Business District from Darling Harbour. Darling Harbour covers 54 hectares and is one of the most ambitious city developments Australia has seen.

Left: The Sydney Aquarium in Darling Harbour is popular with visitors and locals alike. The 15 metre high and 140 metre long aquarium is home to more than 5000 different species of Australian fish in its coral gardens, tidal pools, seal sanctuary and two enormous oceanariums.

Above: At the Aquarium visitors enjoy the mysteries of the deep on the underwater walkway.

Overleaf: One of the finest in the world, Sydney Harbour has 240 kilometres of shoreline. This sparkling body of water, adorned with the Opera House and Harbour Bridge, covers 55 square kilometres.

Opposite, above and right: A bicentennial gift from the Chinese province of Guangdong, the Chinese Gardens at Darling Harbour are the largest and most elaborate of their kind outside China. Dominated by a two-storey pavilion, the traditionally planned gardens embody principles dating back to the fifth century. A serene refuge in the midst of the city, here water trickles under curved bridges and overhanging willows, bamboo rustles in the wind and pagodas offer ideal meditation enclaves. The 12 000 square metre area overflows with lush plant life from flowering apricots and camellias to guava and bamboo and is dramatically highlighted with Chinese art and architecture.

Opposite: Sydney's Central Business District seen from Circular Quay at night. From its beginnings as a convict settlement studded with tents and crossed by bullock tracks, Sydney has grown into a vibrant metropolis. The largest city in the country, covering an area of 12 407 square kilometres, it is the manufacturing, commercial, cultural and sporting centre of the South Pacific.

Left: Dominating the Sydney skyline, the magnificent golden spire of Centrepoint Tower rises 325 metres above sea level. It houses revolving restaurants and an observation platform offering a 360 degree view of the entire Sydney basin, the Blue Mountains and the Tasman Sea. The base of the tower is the centre of the city's retail precinct.

Above: Government House, the official residence of all the governors of New South Walkes since 1845, has many charming aspects. Typically Gothic in style, it replaced the stone residence built for Captain Phillip in 1789 at another site..

Above and opposite: One of Sydney's top shopping venues for jewellery and clothing, the elegant Strand Arcade was built in the 1890s. About 80 specialty shops trade in an 'olde worlde' ambience surrounded by cast-iron roof trusses, stylish galleries, a barrel-vaulted glass roof, stained glass and colourful tessellated tiling.

Opposite and above: Covering an entire city block, the Queen Victoria Building was built between 1893 and 1898 to celebrate the jubilee of the reigning queen. Originally used to house the city markets, today it is an exclusive shopping gallery containing nearly 200 shops. The three-storey Romanesque masterpiece incorporates faithfully restored elements of the architectural grandeur of old, including stained glass, colourful tiling and a magnificent dome of coloured glass.

Above Captain James Cook presides over Hyde Park in the city. Cook, who discovered and charted the east coast, first landed in Botany Bay in 1770.

Opposite: Reminder of days past — an old lantern adorns a building in Macquarie Street. Sydney's premier street for public buildings, it was named after Governor Lachlan Macquarie, who with the help of convict architect Francis Greenway created an elegant, restrained streetscape.

Overleaf: Nestling under sail-like canopies beside the intricate steelwork of the Harbour Bridge, the 150 stalls of the vibrant Rocks Markets draw thousands of bargain hunters every weekend. Wares are varied, including antiques and collectables and handcrafted souvenirs.

Above: The Argyle Arts Centre in the Rocks was built on the site of Sydney's first market garden between 1826 and 1835. Originally bond stores housing rum and many other valuables, the collection of warehouses grouped around a central, cobbled court-yard has been converted into a retail complex of mostly fashion and accessory shops.

Opposite: An open-air arts display at the Rocks. Site of Australia's first European settlement, the Rocks, with its many pubs, lodging houses and brothels gave Sydney the reputation of one of the wildest ports in the world. Nowadays, this area of historical importance with its faithfully restored buildings is the city's outdoor museum and one of its top tourist attractions.

Above: The city's oldest dwelling, Cadman's Cottage in the Rocks, was built in 1816 for the Governor's boat crew and was occupied by John Cadman, the coxswain. In those days the cottage fronted the sea wall where large ships-of-the-line berthed.

Opposite: Hyde Park Barracks, originally built to house 600 male convicts, has had many incarnations: it has housed free settlers, been an insane asylum, a migrant clearing house and also a courthouse. Today the building incorporates a museum on the history of the site and its occupants.

Above: This beautiful art deco building on the western shore of Circular Quay was built during the 1930s to house the Maritime Services Board. It is now the home of the Museum of Contemparary Art which holds regular exhibitions and has become popular with both tourists and the local arts loving community.

Opposite: One of the ten largest museums in the world, the Australian Museum was established in the early 1800s. It features thematically arranged exhibitions covering Australian zoology, mineralogy, anthropology and associated subjects.

Preceding pages, right and below: A combination of fine sculptures and stunning horticulture provide a fascinating setting for photographic opportunities and relaxation at the Botanic Gardens in Sydney.

Opposite: The gardens display a comprehensive selection of native and South Pacific plants as well as collections of flora from other parts of the world. Dedicated in 1816, and reputedly the second oldest botanic gardens in the Southern Hemisphere (after that of Rio de Janeiro), the gardens were the site of Australia's first farm; a small obelisk marks where the first furrows were ploughed in 1788.

Above and opposite: Nestled around Farm Cove, the Royal Botanic Gardens are a tranquil retreat amid the highrises and busy city streets. Major features are the high-tech glass pyramid brimming with tropical plants, Palm Grove, the Pioneer Memorial Garden, the Captain Arthur Phillip Memorial, the formal Rose Garden and the Herbarium.

Previous pages: The Monorail snakes its way through the city, linking Darling Harbour to the city centre. Six automatic trains, operating every few minutes, glide along the one-way route which covers a loop of seven stations. A round trip takes no more than 12 minutes.

Opposite, right and below: Fountains play and coins clatter at Sydney's magnificent Star City Casino. Perched on the Pyrmont peninsula like a massive monument to Mammon, the complex, on a 3.4 hectare site, houses restaurants, theatres, a 5-star hotel, apartments and a giant gaming floor with 1500 poker machines and 160 gaming tables.

Opposite and above: Highlight of Hyde Park, the bronze art deco Archibald Memorial Fountain, designed by French sculptor Sidard, features Apollo, Diana and other mythological figures, rimmed by spitting turtles. It was built, from money bequeathed by francophile John Feltham Archibald, during the 1930s to commemorate the Australian-French Alliance of 1914-18.

Above: A stunning example of art deco architecture, the Anzac War Memorial in Hyde Park is tranquilly mirrored in the Lake of Reflection. Opened in 1934 to commemorate those who served in World War I, it was rededicated in 1984 as a memorial to all Australians who have fought in wars. Inside are two halls — the Hall of Memory and the Hall of Silence.

Opposite: A Gothic masterpiece, the Great Hall of Sydney University was designed and built by Edmund Blackett between 1854 and 1860. The university, the oldest in the city, was founded in 1852.

Opposite: Varied styles of architecture blend to create a charming city skyline — the Queen Victoria Building, the Town Hall and the Carringbush Tower. Opened in 1889, the Town Hall (centre) has a concert hall capable of holding 2200 people.

Above: The Justice and Police Museum at Circular Quay documents the history of crime and punishment in New South Wales from bushrangers to Squizzy Taylor, Australia's answer to Al Capone. Exhibitions cover crimes that have captured the public imagination and a survey of the changing technology and tools of detection used by police.

Right: The Commonwealth Law Courts in Parramatta. A century ago the city was exclusively a farming settlement. Called the Cradle City, it was home to Sydney's first orchard, vineyard, winery and tannery. Today it is a busy centre serving a large industrial and residential district and one of the most important manufacturing regions in the country.

Above and opposite: Sydney's newest bridge, the Anzac Bridge (previously known as the Glebe Island Bridge) was completed in 1996. At 345 metres it is the longest cable-stayed bridge in Australia, using 128 cables to support the 32-metre wide deck. The two spectacular reinforced concrete towers rise 120 metres into the sky.

Opposite and above: Sitting squatly in mid-harbour, the rock island of Fort Denison was originally used to confine convicts in the first few months of settlement in 1788. The fort, built in the 1850s, was to protect Sydney from any attack by the Russian fleet cruising the Pacific during the Crimean War. From 1888 onwards, Fort Denison housed prisoners on short rations, hence the island's nickname of Pinchgut.

Overleaf: Directly over the water from the Opera House, the attractive residential suburb of Kirribilli is home to the official residences of the Prime Minister and Governor General. Here, older apartment blocks mingle with terraces and cottages and quiet streets give a gentle village atmosphere, despite being the most densely developed area of the north shore.

Above: Mingling at Taronga Zoological Gardens. Over 4000 animals reside at the zoo — highlights include the Koala House, orang-utang rainforest, Serpentaria (which is home to native and exotic reptiles, amphibians and invertebrates), and many Australian native animals. The giraffe and elephant enclosures have the best views over Sydney.

Opposite: Horticultural masterpiece — the floral clock in the Taronga Zoological Gardens. Sprawling over a leafy hill on the northern harbour shoreline, this award-winning zoo has panoramic harbour and city skyline views, making it one of the most spectacular zoo settings in the world.

Opposite: Nestled in the middle of lushly designed gardens near the harbour, the Gothic mansion Vaucluse House was once the home of pioneer statesman William Charles Wentworth. Completed in 1829, and now a State Historic Site, it has been faithfully restored as a museum furnished with antiques representing the lifestyle of the nineteenth century.

Above: Tiny weatherboard cottages and minute beaches impart a village atmosphere to Watsons Bay on the harbour side of South Head. The suburb was named after Robert Watson, an early harbour pilot and harbourmaster of the Sydney Port, who was granted land in the formerly isolated spot in 1801.

Right: Classical fluted sandstone columns and imposing statues contrast with the airy, floor-to-ceiling glass interior of the Art Gallery of New South Wales. Permanent collections include some fine Australian art, Aboriginal and New Guinean tribal art, an exquisite Japanese collection as well as a wide range of European art.

Left: Geraniums light up a terrace on one of the many wonderful old buildings in the Rocks. As well as rows of terrace houses, the area has some fine Georgian residences and free-standing sandstone cottages.

Above: Rooftop horizon — looking towards the eastern suburbs from Kings Cross. Once Sydney's most cosmopolitan suburb in its halcyon days of the 1940s when American sailors imbued the area with their own brand of culture, Kings Cross is now Sydney's red light district and backpacker centre.

Opposite: One of the most picturesque suburbs in Sydney, Paddington has steep streets lined with elegantly embellished Victorian terrace-houses. The suburb grew as a village centred around Victoria Barracks and was once very much a working man's estate. Now, totally gentrified, the entire suburb has been placed on the National Trust's classified list of environmental features which should be preserved and is a sought-after place to live.

Above and Opposite: Sydney buzzes on Australia Day, with Tall Ships and other craft filling the harbour with sail. The public holiday commemorates the beginning of white settlement in Australia on 26 January 1788.

Opposite: High, sheer cliffs of The Gap at Watsons Bay drop to the churning ocean below. The wreck of the *Dunbar* in 1857, leaving just one survivor from over one hundred passengers, first earnt this spot its macabre reputation — a reputation reinforced during the 1930s depression when it was the site of an alarmingly high number of suicides.

Above: Perched on the rocks at Parkhill Reserve, North Head, spectators have a bird's eye view of the start of the annual Sydney-to-Hobart yacht race. One of the most spectacular boating races in the world, the start of the race attracts thousands of spectators in their own craft or crowding every garden park and vantage point.

Right: The towering masts of the Tall Ships are an imposing sight on Sydney Harbour during the Australia Day celebrations.

Above: Nicknamed Glamarama, the tiny, perfect little beach of Tamarama in the eastern suburbs is where the beautiful people like to go. The great outdoors forms one of the most important facets of Sydney's lifestyle with stretches of golden beaches fringing the city.

Left: An eclectic collection of apartment blocks overlooking Bondi Bay. Dotting the hillsides of Sydney's inner, ocean and harbourside suburbs, apartment blocks have increased steadily in number over the years. Architectural styles are diverse with early 'shoeboxes' being built in mainly Federation, art deco and Spanish Mission styles.

Opposite: Bondi Beach, Sydney's most famous leisure strip. Good surf, fine white sand and sparkling water combined with great eateries, lively discos and pubs make this sweeping eastern beach one of the city's most popular and vibrant areas. Bondi is an Aboriginal word meaning 'sound of waves breaking on the beach or over rocks'.

Previous pages: Ocean Beach at Manly. Named by Captain Arthur Phillip in 1788 after the manly-looking Aborigines in the area, Manly became a popular seaside resort in the Edwardian era, attracting people from far and wide under the promotional slogan 'Manly, seven miles from Sydney but a thousand miles from care'.

Below: The famous Norfolk pine-lined stretch of Queenscliff, North Steyne and Manly beaches share the same ocean front.

Left: Ferries regularly ply the waters between Circular Quay and Manly Wharf. Suitable for ocean cruising, the enormous *Narrabeen* can carry a thousand passengers.

Opposite: Manly Wharf, gateway to a mixture of old world seaside resort and brash commercial development. The famous Manly Ferries have been carrying passengers to and from here since 1854 and today the ferry ride is still one of Sydney's most scenic forms of transport.

Below: Queenscliff Beach near Manly is one in a long line of beaches stretching to the north. Among the finest in the world, there are 34 ocean beaches in Sydney as well as some delightful stretches on the harbour and river fronts. Early settlers made surprisingly little use of the beaches, public bathing being banned between sunrise and sunset. Not until 1903 were people allowed to bathe in daylight hours. From that day on, Sydney's beaches became the village green of summer social life.

Opposite: Rock baths at Queenscliff. Many of Sydney's ocean beaches have walled pools, providing sanctuary from the sharks patrolling the surrounding waters.

Right: Surf culture is an important part of Sydney's life and some of the finest surfing in the world can be experienced at Sydney's magnificent surfing beaches. The most popular places to catch a wave include Bondi, Tamarama, Manly, Narrabeen, Mona Vale, Bilgola, Collaroy, Cronulla, Long Reef and Palm Beach.

Below: Tebbutt's Observatory, Windsor, was built in 1863 for the distinguished astronomer John Tebbutt (1834-1916) who discovered the comet which bears his name.

Right: Stained glass glows richly in St Matthew's Church of England in Windsor. Designed by convict architect Francis Greenway in 1817 and completed in 1821 it is said to be the second oldest Church of England in the country. Built entirely out of hand-made sandstone bricks it originally had a shingle roof which was later replaced with copper.

Opposite: The Macquarie Arms, Windsor, was built at Governor Macquarie's request and opened in 1811. The first licensee was emancipist Robert Fitzgerald. The third oldest town in Australia, Windsor is situated on broad flats overlooking the Hawkesbury River 56 kilometres north-west of Sydney. First settled in 1794 and called Green Hills, its name was changed by Governor Macquarie in 1810.

Opposite: The Parramatta River winds through the city of Parramatta. It was this waterway that encouraged early settlers to establish farms out of the main Sydney settlement. Founded in 1788 by Governor Phillip, Parramatta, situated 24 kilometres west of the city, was the second settlement established in New South Wales. Now a bustling city in its own right, it remains a place of great historical interest.

Left: Elizabeth Farm House, built in 1793 by famous farming pioneer John Macarthur, is the oldest surviving building in Australia and was the prototype of the country's farming architecture, with an extended roof providing shelter for verandahs on all sides. The farm was the site of the earliest experiments in merino wool production.

Below: The luxurious RiverCat takes passengers along the Parramatta River, an arm of Sydney Harbour.

Opposite: Hambledon Cottage was originally commissioned by John Macarthur for his children's governess on her retirement. Open for public inspection, it is charmingly furnished in period style.

Below: Old Government House, Parramatta, was designed for Governor Macquarie and completed in 1816. It incorporates the house built in 1799 for Governor Hunter.

Right: Springtime in Parramatta Park.

Above and opposite: Sydney's main water supply, the Warragamba Dam is 116 metres high and can hold 2.1 million cubic metres of water. Part of the Warragamba River upstream from Penrith is held back by a massive 350-metre long wall to create one of the largest dams in the world for metropolitan water supply. Sydney is serviced by a complex system of six major dams, service reservoirs, pumping stations and pipelines. Two major rivers have been developed as sources of supply. There are dams in the Upper Nepean river system on the Cataract, Cordeaux and Avon Rivers and on the Nepean itself. The Warragamba River, fed by the Wollondilly, Nattai, Coxs and Kowmung Rivers, has been harnessed by the mighty Warragamba Dam. The Upper Nepean catchment area covers 900 square kilometres and the Warragamba or Lake Burrajong catchment, 9000 square kilometres. The sixth major dam is on the Woronora River.

Opposite: The Three Sisters at Katoomba in the Blue Mountains. According to Aboriginal legend, three sisters, Meenhi, Wimlah and Gunedoo were turned to stone by a tribal witchdoctor to protect them from three warriors, who, being in love with the girls had decided to take them by force. Unfortunately the witchdoctor was killed in the ensuing battle and no one has been able to break the spell and turn the sisters back into human form.

Above: Hanging Rock looms out above dense vegetation in the Blue Mountains National Park. Rising to the west of Sydney, the Blue Mountains form part of the Great Dividing Range which extends along the entire east coast of the continent. It is an area of sheer grandeur where sparkling streams plunge down steep cliffs, glens and gorges, while tall timbers, ferny grottoes and natural rock amphitheatres stand before an awesome backdrop of rugged mountains.

Above: Riding above a carpet of cloud, the Scenic Skyway at Katoomba soars 300 metres from one clifftop to another. Constructed in 1958, the Skyway was the first horizontal passenger-carrying ropeway in the Southern Hemisphere.

Right: Sylvia Falls splash into the fern-filled gullies of the Valley of Waters in the Blue Mountains National Park. Covering an area of 100 865 hectares, it is the second largest national park in the state.

Overleaf: Cascades and froth at Weeping Rock, Wentworth Falls. Mysterious blue mists shroud the valley, creating ever-changing patterns of green, mauve, blue and purple.

Opposite: Medlow Bath's most famous landmark, the Hydromajestic Hotel, with its sweeping Megalong Valley views and unique federation-come-art deco architecture was one of the first holiday establishments operating in the area. It was originally a health resort, advertised as a 'hydropathic' centre, offering massage, sun, mud and sand baths. In the early 1900s the Blue Mountain region was promoted for the quality of its air which was said to have health-giving properties.

Above: Yester Grange, a charming Victorian country house at Wentworth Falls. Built in 1870 for John See, a former Premier of New South Wales, today the historic home operates as an arts centre and has been restored and furnished in the period.

Above: Rose Lindsay Cottage, now a beautifully restored guesthouse, stands in a forest of towering gums and native wildflower garden at Faulconbridge.

Opposite: The sheer cliffs of the Blue Mountains are a rock climber's paradise. Here, high precipices rise from thickly wooded valleys and deep gorges, making much of the terrain inaccessible except to skilled bushwalkers and mountaineers. Seemingly impenetrable, these rugged sandstone ridges proved a barrier to expansion that defeated the colony's most able explorers for almost 25 years.

Opposite: Rainforest and treeferns border the sparkling Leura Falls. The elevated sandstone plateau that makes up the Blue Mountains has been chiselled and eroded over millennia by the creeks and rivers that plunge down sheer rockfaces and tumble over fallen stones into gullies below.

Above: Long rays of autumn sunlight gild the deciduous trees at Leura in the Blue Mountains. At its heyday in the 1920s, today Leura brims with restaurants, craft, gift and antique shops.

Above: Winter snow at Blackheath. In the late 1800s the Blue Mountains became fashionable with wealthy members of Sydney society, several of whom built mansions there as mountain retreats.

Opposite: The famous Zig Zag Railway puffs its way over stone viaducts and through cuttings and tunnels near Lithgow. Built between 1866 and 1869 to overcome the problem of a very precipitous descent from the Blue Mountains to the Western Plains beyond, this breathtaking stretch of railway was regarded as an engineering masterpiece.

Opposite: Visitors peruse the Tourist Information Centre at Mittagong. A popular holiday destination, the Southern Highlands district comprises about 280 000 hectares of picturesque mountain country. The main centres are Mittagong, Bowral, Moss Vale, Berrima and Bundanoon and scenic attractions in the area include the Fitzroy Falls, Kangaroo Valley and Wombeyan Caves.

Above: Autumn tones at Mittagong, south of Sydney. Glorious landscapes, towering forests, bracing air and a fascinating history provide a unique atmosphere throughout the lofty plateau country known as the Southern Highlands.

Opposite: Wattamolla Falls in the Royal National Park, south of Sydney. The oldest national park in Australia and one of the oldest in the world, it contains superb bushland and river scenery, covering nearly 15 000 hectares. Established in 1879 as an acclimatisation zoo for animals and game birds, today the park is home to many native animals, including a colony of lyrebirds, as well as a herd of free-range deer.

Left: Perching on boats and wharf piles or gliding across calm waters, the Australian Pelican is one of the most evocative of all waterbirds. Seen here on sparkling Lake Illawarra, south of Sydney, pelicans are found in the shallows of coastal or inland waters. Large birds, with a wingspan of 2.5 metres, they have enormous bills and bill pouches used in securing food as well as for cooling the birds in hot weather when they open their bills and rapidly flutter the skin.

Above: Frolicking in Wattamolla Creek in the Royal National Park. Picnickers, hikers and nature lovers can enjoy the heath-covered sandstone plateau, ferny glades, wildflowers, giant trees and patches of dense rainforest the park offers as well as some of the best of the southern ocean beaches.

Above: Australia's first prefabricated lighthouse gleams whitely at Belmore Basin on the southern breakwater at Wollongong. No longer in use, it has been replaced by a more modern one on Flagstaff Hill. Wollongong Harbour is the only point on the east coast of Australia with two lighthouses.

Opposite: Wollongong, south of Sydney, was named for the Aboriginal word 'hard ground near water'. Fine beaches are scattered along the rugged, craggy Illawarra coast, which stretches from Sydney, south to Bateman's Bay, offering some of the best scenery in the state.

Opposite: Mt Kiera Lookout offers panoramic views over Wollongong and the southern coast. The third largest city in New South Wales and the seventh largest in Australia, Wollongong is a popular tourist centre with fine surfing beaches. It is home to the Port Kembla Steelworks, the largest industrial complex in the Southern Hemisphere.

Above: The small enclosed Wollongong Harbour is refuge for a major commercial fishing fleet and many pleasure craft.

Overleaf: Wooded slopes tumble from the spine of Bouddi Peninsula to peaceful beaches along the deeply indented coast of Bouddi National Park. The state's first marine park, it is situated along a narrow coastal strip on the northern entrance to Broken Bay and covers 1147 hectares of wildflower-studded coastal heath, stands of eucalypts and coastal rainforest.

Opposite: The Entrance on the Central Coast bursts into life over summer months when holidaymakers arrive to enjoy the boating, fishing, swimming and surfing. The thriving town sits on the south shore of Tuggerah Lake, overlooking the narrow strip of water separating lake from ocean.

Above: Snorkelling the waters of the north coast. Sydney Harbour and the surrounding coastline have many great spots for exploring marine life, reefs, sponge gardens and wrecks.

Above: Pelicans patiently await tasty morsels at The Entrance. The Central Coast area is Sydney's holiday playground, offering endless stretches of pounding surf or tranquil water beaches, unspoiled bush and mountain scenery, rural valleys, sparkling waterfalls and humming tourist towns.

Opposite: Enjoying the peace and solitude of Myall Lakes National Park, north of Sydney. One of the least spoilt and tranquil coastal areas in the state, the park encompasses a system of forest fringed waterways covering more than 10 000 hectares and separated by windswept sand dunes from the ocean beaches.

Previous pages: Sunset streaks the sky over Brisbane Water, West Gosford. Boating, fishing and all watersports are popular on this large expanse of calm water that stretches from the coast inland to Gosford.

Opposite: Boating enthusiasts enjoy the tranquillity of Berowra Waters, an arm of the Hawkesbury River. The longest river on the east coast, it has its mouth at Broken Bay, just north of Palm Beach, and winds through magnificent countryside, forming a quarter circle around Sydney. It is navigable for 113 kilometres for large boats and 137 for smaller craft.

Left: A holiday mecca for many thousands of people, the Central Coast offers great swimming, fishing and boating on its many sparkling surf beaches and quiet waterways. Just lazing on the warm golden sands is a popular alternative.

Following pages: A hive of aquatic activity at the picturesque settlement of Brooklyn where the railway line crosses the Hawkesbury River. A plaque in the park commemorates Captain Phillip's exploration of the area in 1788.

Opposite: With a reputation for being the most beautiful river on the Australian continent, the Hawkesbury river travels through majestic unspoiled bush and sandstone scenery to picturesque rural surrounds.

Below: The Colo, Wollemi, Wolgan and Capertree Rivers have carved a maze of interlocking cliff-edged canyons and gorges in the extremely rugged Wollemi National Park north-west of Sydney. With an area of 450 000 hectares it is the second largest national park in New South Wales (after Kosciuszko).

Right: Protected bays, rolling surf and tranquil rivers are all within easy reach of most Sydneysiders who grow up with fond memories of aquatic holidays.

Sheltered beaches, rolling pasture and rugged headlands near Kiama on the southern coast of New South Wales. Ideal for swimming and fishing, the south coast offers some of the most magnificent scenery in the state.

INDEX